UPSCALE YOUR

VIRTUAL ASSISTANT

BUSINESS

Written by Jaimie Skultety

UPSCALE YOUR VIRTUAL ASSISTANT BUSINESS

Fast Track Your Way to a Successful Virtual Assistant Business, Establish Your Credibility, Expertise, and Personal Brand.

Have Joyful Workdays—when you WANT to work—and Make More Money than you ever thought possible!

By Jaimie Skultety

© 2014 Jaimie Skultety

To learn more, visit www.UpscaleYourVirtualAssistantBusiness.com

Testimonials

"Jaimie provides excellent service to all of her clients, including those needing rush jobs. She stays on top of everything and is very organized. I have been on Jaimie's team since 2012 and love the fact that she communicates very well with her clients and her peers. She willingly shares her expertise regarding the Virtual Assistant field and I have learned a lot from her. She will always to lend a helping hand. Her knowledge of social media is beyond belief. I have learned from various sources, but it's amazing how she constantly gives me tips and tricks on how to take things to the next level for clients as well as for my own business."
Richard Rinyai, Virtual Assistant
Owner, Virtual Office Guy
www.virtualofficeguy.com

"Jaimie and I are in the same profession. I can't say enough about her. Her guidance and advice has helped me in every way to grow my business. She is extremely knowledgeable in social media and she has a fabulous background in processes and systems. This, along with her kind and patient demeanor, makes her an absolute winner in my book and for sure she would be in yours."
Stephanie Scharer, Virtual Assistant

"Jaimie is an absolute superstar at being a virtual assistant. Her depth of knowledge and out-of-box ideas adds major value to businesses. I assist Jaimie with some of her client assignments and highly recommend her for her creativity, being reliable and her excellent work. She loves what she does and you can absolutely see that every time in the quality of the job she does."
Haja, Virtual Assistant

"Jaimie is the best VA I've ever had. She is the perfect role model for VAs. When you look up "virtual assistant" in the dictionary, I think you'll find a picture of Jaimie. Just kidding of course, but she is the best. Jaimie really understands what a business owner needs. I never have to worry about her completing an assignment or project on time and within budget. Jaimie acts with integrity and makes each client feel like her most important client. She is trustworthy and has great customer service skills. Many of my clients comment about her responsiveness and her friendly yet professional style. She has enhanced my company brand."
Beverly Harvey, Client
Owner, Harvey Careers
www.HarveyCareers.com

"Jaimie's passion for making business development happen is apparent in everything she does. I have been a small business owner since 1993 and appreciate that Jaimie is a rare find in that she thinks strategically and tactically, positions rapidly, and executes flawlessly. Jaimie understands my strategy and has saved my company time and money by taking appropriate initiatives to streamline processes. I recommend her highly for any small business owner who wants to proactively build a business!"
Annette Baron, Client
Owner, Proposal Architect
www.proposal-architect.com

Acknowledgements

To all the Virtual Assistants who have come before me and paved the way for my journey…This VA community is one which I have found to be supportive, helpful, and resourceful. It is gratifying and inspiring for me to be in the company of other professionals who are as passionate about this industry as I am.

To all the Virtual Assistants who are just beginning their journey, you can trust that you are embarking on a most rewarding and exceptional career. Welcome to the Community!

Many more people than one realizes play an important role in the life of an entrepreneur, and often it is not until we sit down to think about it that we recognize how these people have helped us get where we are. In acknowledging who these people are in my life and indulging in a comprehensive and heart-felt display of gratitude to them, I hope my readers will notice too who in their lives have been an inspiration and who will be part of their journey to becoming a successful Virtual Assistant.

PROFESSIONAL DEDICATIONS

To all my Coaches, Mastermind Leaders, and Group Members who have helped me in shaping my business…far too many people to list here, but special thanks are in order for Anna Losito, Mande White (www.mandewhite.com), Annette James (http://influentialentrepreneuracademy.com), and Danielle Keister (http://administrativeconsultantsassoc.com/).

To Julie Jansen (www.juliejansen.net) & Fran Asaro (www.thriveanyway.com) …who both suggested Virtual Assistance as the perfect career for me to transition into when the company I worked for became victim of the economy crash in early 2009. With an infant son at the time, the option to work from home was a "no-brainer." I am eternally grateful that both Julie and Fran—who don't know each other—offered this suggestion, and for the "vision" they sparked for me.

To my amazing team of subcontractors and right-hand partners...I am proud to say I have selected people for my team that have exhibited amazing talent, skills, initiative, and dedication. It took me a while to be able to justify and to afford the expense of being a VA who has a VA (or now, a team of VA's), but truly, it has been **the most worthwhile investment** in growing my business. As VA's, we insist to our potential clients that they need to delegate in order for their business to grow, and I wholeheartedly agree. My team has supported both me and my clients, and their assistance has opened up additional opportunities for expanding my business, such as writing this book and working on new products and services.

To my clients, past, present, and future, long-term, and short-term...I have clients who have worked with me since my first weeks in business and continue to this day. Although we've never met and we may never get to meet in person, we have a bond which is just as special to me as my personal friends and family. We share a passion for being entrepreneurs, and they have respected me at a level far beyond "assistant." I know without question they see me as their equal, and they have encouraged and inspired me in so many ways. I also wish to acknowledge those former clients who recognized we were not a good "fit" to continue our work together—I am grateful we were able to "let go," retaining honor and respect for each other.

PERSONAL DEDICATIONS

To my Advisory Committee (my mom and stepdad)…I have been fortunate enough to have grown up in a household where my mother, who was single during most of my "informative" years, owned her own Interior Design business. She won several awards, was featured in national design magazines, local newspapers, and although she owned brick-and-mortar stores, she often worked from inside her home office. She was there for me as a mom, but also demonstrated a beautiful example of how to be a successful entrepreneur **and** raise a child, and to do both of these things really well. But the fact that she managed to accomplish and balance both of these things and that she could feel so incredibly fulfilled in these endeavors was more inspirational to me than I realized at the time. Thank you for that gift. Thank you for being an exceptional mom to me—and amazing grandma to Spencer.

To my stepdad, Barry…who has been in my life since 1994, bringing with him not only my amazing sister, Amy, and brother, Paul, and their beautiful spouses and children, but his business acumen and insights, and his ability—through his reviews and edits—to take my words and my context to a level beyond that I could ever achieve on my own. So, Barry…thank you for marrying my mom and making her happy for over 20 years, thank you for being a generous and loving stepfather, and thank you for your commitment that my business be as successful as it can be. You always have my best interest at heart.

To my Daddy…You have always been the most loving and supportive father any girl could ask for. I love you for far too many reasons to share here (the book would end up being a thousand pages long for goodness sake!) But I KNOW you know how much I love you and, as long as you know this, I am complete.

To learn more, visit www.UpscaleYourVirtualAssistantBusiness.com

To my Aunt Ellen and Uncle Ivan…You have been here for me throughout my entire life in every way imaginable, and I am eternally grateful and appreciative beyond what you know. Words could never express the depth of what's in my heart for you.

To Grandma and Grandpa…Simply put, I miss you **every single day**. I am so grateful that I was able to share my life with you all the way into my 40's. I wish you could be here to see me achieve even greater success. I will carry your love in my heart…always.

To my husband, Steve…who has supported, encouraged and believed in me. You have partnered so beautifully with me in raising our son and managing our household. I love sharing my life with you. Thank you for supporting me in being an entrepreneur. But most of all, thank you for being a wonderful father.

Most importantly, to my son, Spencer…You are the sweetest, kindest, most loving, and thoughtful young man. It is the greatest privilege of my life to be your mom. **You are the inspiration for everything I do. I hope to inspire you, just as my mom inspired me.** And **so** the legacy continues!

Table of Contents

To learn more, visit www.UpscaleYourVirtualAssistantBusiness.com

To learn more, visit www.UpscaleYourVirtualAssistantBusiness.com

Introduction

This book is primarily written for new, aspiring, and struggling Virtual Assistants, but will serve also to provide valuable insights and ideas for all Virtual Assistants. My intention is that you learn *how* to become an *effective* and *exceptional* Virtual Assistant and *where* to find clients and *how* to keep them.

In the pages of this book, you can count on me to share what I myself have learned that has enabled me to have a successful Virtual Assistant business.

When I started, I was putting in 16-18 hour days, but I am pleased to report that I now work the hours I choose, have a wonderful client roster and a six-figure annual income. I say this not to brag, but to share with you what truly is possible.

There are tricks of the trade I wish someone had shared with me when I was first starting out. I will be teaching several of these in this book, so you won't need to spend long days as I did.

Please go to my website—there's a link at the footer of each page—and learn more about how I can assist you to avoid the pitfalls I had to experience and how I can help you fast-track your Virtual Assistant business to success.

What is a Virtual Assistant?

A **Virtual Assistant**—typically abbreviated to VA—is generally self-employed, works remotely from a home office, and provides professional, administrative, and/or marketing/social media assistance to one or more clients.

If you have strong administrative skills and you have a passion for this type of work, there is every opportunity to meet your personal and professional goals. It can be either a full- or part-time business. I have subcontractor VA's who work for me part-time simply to supplement their household income.

It's a wonderful and still rapidly growing industry—a rewarding career choice on so many levels. Best of all is that you are your own boss! Not a day goes by that I don't acknowledge how amazing it is that I don't have to ask for vacation time, a sick day, time off to care for my sick son; I can choose to go shopping or to the spa or hair salon when I want. It's a different world when you work for yourself.

Whatever your age, if you have the skills and learn how to market yourself, you can translate this into a successful VA business—I started mine two days after my 40th birthday, and I am so grateful I was driven to this career choice.

Section 1—Getting Started

*"The Secret to Getting Ahead
is Getting Started"*

~ Mark Twain

A Computer and Fax Does Not Make You a Virtual Assistant

There are a few items to mention as we get started. First and foremost, I want to highlight that the amount of time that you will need to dedicate to getting your business off the ground will depend on your income goals and desire to succeed. The hard lesson I learned when starting out is that business does not come just because you're open for business. If you don't have a ready source of clients, there is much more you will need to do than you might imagine. I will be covering this in the following pages.

Basic Essentials

- ○ **Computer:** Either desktop or laptop; it could be a Mac or PC. I would strongly recommend a new or relatively new computer from the outset—this way you start out your business *fresh* without "garbed-up" history. Personally I prefer a laptop PC, as I like to take work with me on the go. There are excellent programs that provide access to data when travelling. I recommend too that you have an external hard drive *with a large memory*, so that you can back up all your files, which you should do on a weekly basis. An online backup system is advisable too in case your external hard drive becomes corrupted or is lost due to flood, fire, or theft. I use Carbonite (http://carbonite.com/); it performs continuous backup throughout the day and saves all of my data "in the cloud." Documents in the cloud can be accessed at any time from any computer on the internet. This way all files—yours and clients'—are permanently safe.

- ○ **Printer/Scanner/Fax:** An all-in-one printer/scanner/fax is compact and perfectly adequate. I use RingCentral (http://www.ringcentral.com/), which enables me to send and receive faxes through my computer; and they also provide a toll-free phone/fax number.

o **Software:** This includes both stand-alone and online software. An example of stand-alone software would be Microsoft Office. I believe in upgrading and updating any time a new program comes out. However, before making a new purchase, it is advisable to wait for beta testing to be completed and read the reviews. Having the latest and greatest definitely impresses clients and it will always help to improve the overall running of your business.

An example of online software would be a customer relations management program or database programs such as Microsoft Outlook and ACT, or could be as basic as Excel. I use Microsoft Outlook for my own business but have several clients who use ACT. (http://www.act.com). ACT has a web-based program as well as a server-based program. A server-based program enables both me and my client to access the same content and we synchronize. Throughout the day, the computer continually updates the software and the main database with everything I and my client independently input.

o **Accounting Software:** Whether or not you do your own books, you will need accounting software. I use QuickBooks and prefer the online version, as I have an accountant who manages my books each month. I used to do the books myself, but as the volume of my business increased, it was one of the tasks I happily and easily delegated. With QuickBooks Online (http://www.quickbooksonline.com), my accountant can log into my system *from his office*, update my checkbook, and manage the monthly reconciliation.

o **Client Payment Systems:** You should have a merchant or credit card processing account, a PayPal account, and a check-by-phone account. This way you cover all bases. Not having the ability to pay you in the manner desired can lose you potential clients.

O **Industry Memberships:** For early visibility, I recommend joining International Virtual Assistants Association (www.IVAA.org) and Administrative Consultants Association (http://administrativeconsultantsassoc.com/).

These memberships add to your credibility as a VA and can provide you with direct leads. Potential clients view completed member bios and contact those VA's whose services and skills match the criteria they are looking for. While it would be very nice to *sit back* and wait for such prospects, **don't**…these same potential clients are contacting other VA's too!

Another benefit, especially with IVAA, is a platform called "RFP," which is Request for Proposal. Potential clients submit that they're looking for Virtual Assistants with particular skills. If you are signed up to receive these RFP's and possess those skills, you will be sent an email and have the opportunity to respond to the potential client directly, setting out the reasons why you are a perfect fit and how you will accomplish what they need.

These sites have been successful for my business, and I consider them well worth the approximate $100 investment per membership annually. Make sure your profile is complete and, importantly, that it is updated as you acquire new skills.

O **Training Programs:** Let's say you have strong skills in Microsoft Word, but need a brush-up on Excel or PowerPoint. In most cases sufficient training can be found free on the internet, but in some cases an investment in a certified course may be worth the cost for the benefit of the added skills you will acquire and the extra prestige that certification brings.

Basic Skills

What are some of the basic skills needed to be considered a "good" VA?

- *O* **Strong computer based skills**: Obviously, you will need to be proficient at typing and data entry: fast and *accurate*. At a minimum, you have to know Microsoft Office, including Word and Excel. (If there is a task within these programs you are required to do but don't know how, you will find instructions in a Google search or on YouTube.) You should familiarize yourself with other popular software programs and have the ability to learn them quickly, if called upon to use them.

- *O* **Organizational and multi-tasking skills:** To manage several clients at a time with different business models, you must have innate organizational talent and know how to use technology to create systems and processes.

- *O* **Project Management skills:** You must be proficient at managing every aspect of a project from start to finish, including managing team members, subcontractors, and vendors. It is essential to be detail-oriented. Know when to report updates and progress to your client.

- *O* **People skills:** As a Virtual Assistant, you will work with many different clients, and *their* clients. Each will bring their own personality, mindset, business model, and expectations. Your "people" skills will be tested on a regular basis. To be a Virtual Assistant, you need to be patient, have an even temper, and maintain professionalism in all your communications; you should be able to articulate responses

To learn more, visit www.UpscaleYourVirtualAssistantBusiness.com

in a way that immediately "disarms" your client from feeling "defensive."

○ **Business Management skills:** A background in business is helpful. If you have worked for five or more years in an administrative capacity, you will have undoubtedly observed and absorbed business factors that will be of value to you as a Virtual Assistant and to your clients. You will benefit from reading a business management book.

○ **Creativity skills:** Being able to innovate, to introduce fresh ideas, to systematize your clients' processes, to think critically, makes you more valuable as a Virtual Assistant.

○ **Resourcefulness/Internet savvy:** Resources abound! Know where and how to access them. You are of extra value to your clients if you can resolve their problem quickly. Understand how to effectively navigate the internet to find solutions, and always be willing to share new tools and programs with your clients.

○ **Communication skills**: As a Virtual Assistant, you need to be a good communicator, a good listener who responds directly, fully, and clearly to the subject matter, without digressing, and in a way that is easy for the listener or reader to understand and assimilate.

○ **Writing skills:** This comes next to last, but it is the most basic, yet also the greatest downfall for so many Virtual Assistants. Most of your communication will be in writing, and some will be forwarded by your clients to their clients. You may be writing blogs and articles for social media and newsletters. If your writing is not consistently of high quality, you will likely be fired, even if your work otherwise is satisfactory. You must type accurately, punctuate, spell and use grammar correctly, use paragraphs appropriately, and maintain a single font type, color and size within a communication unless variation is used for emphasis purposes.

Most programs have some form of "checks" that indicate where errors have occurred. Always look at these and always proof what you have written before sending it. If necessary, study a grammar book—it can all be learned, *and it might make the difference to your career as a Virtual Assistant.* Keep it on your desk and refer to it whenever you have doubts, or use Google.

- *o* **Social media skills:** This comes last as it is only an essential skill if you will be offering social media services to clients. If that will be the case, then you really have to be very advanced in your knowledge of all the social media platforms, their workings, and benefits. It takes considerable time to build up this knowledge and to understand what content, when and where to post.

If you have additional skills, emphasize these on your website.

Branding Yourself

How are you going to stand out? What's going to make a difference in your being successful, regardless of the competition?

- *o* **A clever business name:** If you are starting out providing only task-based services to clients, you can be considered a "Virtual Assistant." This conventionally has been *the* term used for our industry, and at the time of writing, many clients still recognize it as such. However, people I respect within the industry are moving away from this term, as its connotation is considered **limited** with respect to broader services a client might benefit from or expect these days. The trend is developing towards terms such as "Virtual

Administrative Consultant" for those of us who are highly experienced, who take on projects beyond task-based assignments, and are *proactive* and capable of contributing to the growth of a client's business. I make this point with regards to your thinking when you are deciding on a business name.

My original business name was *A Virtual Assistant 4 You*. I chose the name solely for Search Engine Optimization (SEO) purposes. I did get a substantial number of potential clients who found my business in a web search, so I can't say it hurt to have "Virtual Assistant" within the name. However, in view of the trend I have explained and of the broader range of services I now offer, I changed my business name in 2013 to *Upscale Your Business,* which has also worked very well! It enables me justifiably to charge clients a higher fee too. Perception is key...*starting off with a dynamic name that communicates your value will help for the long-term.*

○ **Your logo and colors:** What colors should you choose? We all have different preferences for colors, so my advice is to pick your favorites. Pick colors you will love to look at **all the time**. I choose to go with blue and orange—I really like those two colors together, and it makes me feel happy every time I look at my website. All your marketing materials and social media platforms will also be designed around the colors you choose. Be sure the colors translate well into easily readable print. As they will be your signature for years to come, you won't want to regret your choice. If you are not comfortable making the logo and color selections yourself, it is advisable to work with a graphic designer. Fiverr (www.fiverr.com) will be your least expensive resource for this.

- **Creative tagline:** In a succinct one-liner, what would you want to convey to your audience? Whatever your business name, your tagline should convey exactly what it is that you do, how you solve a problem for your clients. Mine is *"Stress Relief for Overworked Entrepreneurs."*

   When conceived and created properly a really good tagline reinforces your brand's message and helps connect an idea with your audience. Think of a tagline as an opportunity to articulate your differentiation, express your personality or convey some other important brand quality. You can use your tagline on your website and within your marketing materials.

   Here's a resource to learn more about how to create an effective tagline: http://www.hingemarketing.com/library/article/elements_of_a_successful_brand_2_the_tagline.

- **Express your personality:** On your website, incorporate attractive design elements, which express your personality, including professional and relevant graphics and fonts. You can even create an entire theme. If you like octopuses, for example, as a representation of multi-tasking, find octopus images to "sprinkle" in different poses throughout the site...a fun theme, while being relevant too.

- **Your business email address:** A dot com email address is better suited to a business than a Gmail, AOL or Yahoo account. When you set up your website, have your web hosting company provide you with one or two email addresses. For example, I have jaimie@upscaleyourbusiness.com and info@upscaleyourbusiness.com.

Shout It From the Rooftops

So the seeds are planted. How will you now start to find clients? Let's look at some examples of "Shout it from the rooftops."

- ℴ **People in your immediate circles:** The first step is to let the people in your immediate circles know you're creating this new business venture. If you have children at school, take every opportunity to share the news with parents you know from the school. At the nail salon, your hairdresser, supermarket, bank, dry cleaner, coffee shop, and just about anywhere that you go on a regular basis, try to work it into the conversation with the people you know there. For example, you might say: "I'm so lucky that I work for myself and I can get my nails done on my own time since I work from home." Mentioning this in a casual matter-of-fact way will invite people to ask about the type of business you have that gives you the opportunity to work from home. It's a perfect opening.

- ℴ **New people you meet:** Whenever the opportunity arises, ask people you meet what they do for a living, and they will likely ask the same. When you tell them you're a Virtual Assistant or Virtual Administrative Consultant, they invariably find this fascinating and ask thoughtful and insightful questions. You educate people, while at the same time you are marketing yourself. You never know, a client may result!

- ℴ **Share your story and show your passion for what you do**: Be willing to share what has happened in your life and/or work that brought you to the decision to transition into this business. What in your life has opened up for you to be able to embark on this new venture?

- *O* **Hand out your business cards:** This small investment has potential for large distribution. Give everyone a card. If you start telling people about your new business before you have cards, keep a list of names and make sure to circle back with them and give them a card.

- *O* **Ask for referrals:** "While *you* may not need my services, you might know someone who *does*, so here's my card, and I'd be grateful if you'd pass it along." You could even offer a referral fee, $xx for every so many hours a client signs up with you as a result of their introduction.

Where and How to Network

Attend groups, meetings, and events. Know your niche—who you serve and who your target market is—and focus your efforts accordingly.

- *O* **MeetUp.com:** (www.meetup.com) As the website name suggests, these are meetings where people with similar interests or careers get together, for the most part informally. Think of it as a "club." In most cases, there is no membership fee. Type in your zip code on the website and search for MeetUp groups, using relevant keywords such as "small business" or "entrepreneurs." If you specialize in working with a particular profession, you could type that profession in the keyword search**.** Occasionally there are groups with strict membership policies, but most have open membership.

  Fill out your bio, making sure it's *complete*, find out when and where meetings are being held (some require an RSVP), put them on your calendar…**and GO!** During my first six months as a VA, I made it my **business** to attend as many MeetUps as I could fit into a week. There are breakfast, lunch, happy hour, and evening MeetUps…more than enough options for whatever times a schedule permits!

O **Chamber of Commerce:** Usually they offer a breakfast or luncheon. One of the benefits is the membership directory with everyone's contact information. It's a great tool to use in connecting: "I met you at the Chamber of Commerce breakfast. I will contact you if I or my clients have a need for your service. In the meantime, please keep me in mind for your administrative needs."

O **Integrating:** For MeetUp groups, Chamber of Commerce meetings, and similar groups, in order to make connections, you have to be confident about introducing yourself to other attendees. In some cases, groups can be "cliquey," so if you are uncomfortable injecting yourself into that kind of atmosphere, you will not benefit. Where there are membership fees, ask if you can attend a first meeting for free to see if it is a good fit for you. Also, be sure you see an opportunity for visibility within the group. You may find the group already has other VA members, so you might be in direct competition with an established "go to" person…people can be quite territorial.

O **Trade shows:** Attend local business trade shows and get to know some exhibitors. Tell them what you do. Explore ways you might collaborate and partner up to help promote each other's businesses.

I decided to exhibit at a trade show early on, and fortunately it proved to be a worthwhile investment, a lot of fun too. I made great connections. Over time, the one client I got from the event more than paid for my costs, plus ultimately referred a friend who also became a client.

I had giveaways and prizes at my booth, though—as often will be the case—more people were interested in these than in what I was offering. Some trade show visitors attend with the sole intention of seeking new business rather than to purchase products or services that exhibitors are selling. Take the good with the bad and hope that some opportunity presents itself, *whether you exhibit or just attend*!

O **Elevator speech:** Have a snappy one-liner that conveys exactly what you do. I have a couple. My first is a simple: "I take your to-do-list and get it done." My more effective one is: "I help busy entrepreneurs free up time in their day so they can make more money in their business." Invariably this prompts the response: "How do you do that?" From this point we are engaged in conversation.

O **Offer to speak at an event:** If you have the right kind of personality and don't mind getting up in front of a group of people, a quality speech with strong, helpful content—if possible including a PowerPoint presentation—will get you noticed and create buzz. Attendees will come up afterwards to congratulate you and good connections with potential clients will develop.

Website Basics—Elements to Include

What are clients looking for when they go to your website? If you have this question answered and remain focused on the answer, it will help enormously in the development of your website. Don't fall into the trap of including only what appeals to you. Here are the important basics.

O **Have your website ready before you start to promote your business:** Otherwise you will have to rely solely on referrals. My recommendation would be to create your website using WordPress (www.wordpress.com), which is the firm favorite of most Virtual Assistants and small businesses. You *can* do this on your own, but because of the need for your website to *immediately impress*, if you can afford to do so, I would advise hiring a professional website designer and writer. Elance (www.elance.com) is a site where you can get bids from website designers (indeed all types of freelance businesses) and find excellent pricing—but make sure to review several website samples before hiring anyone. You must work closely with your designer to create a style and text that reflects your personality and targets the needs of your audience. Using WordPress, you will be able add/change text, graphics, and images at any time.

O **Testimonials:** If you are starting out, add your profile to LinkedIn and ask former employers and co-workers for their "Recommendations." Request their permission to use those as Testimonials for your website.

O **Frequently Asked Questions or FAQ's:** Study other Virtual Assistant websites and gather ideas for frequently asked questions. What are the questions being asked and what are the best answers? Don't copy from other websites, be creative, and devise answers that are appropriate to your business.

O **The services you provide:** Detail your services in full or give a general overview in a list format. Invite special requests too.

O **YouTube video intro:** I had one on my first site, titled "Meet Your VA." It may seem presumptive to say, "I'm your Virtual Assistant, so let me tell you about me." But clients like to know you a little, to see your face, hear your voice, and get a feel for your personality, since in many cases they won't meet you in person. The video should be short, maximum three minutes, and provide a nice introduction to your business. My video got a high volume of views and people told me they loved it.

○ **Social media button and links:** Have your Facebook page, your Twitter profile, your LinkedIn, and Google+ profiles on your website, and check that all the links work. You may even want to include Pinterest.

○ **Contact information:** A toll-free number, email address, and office hours (time zone) are the minimum requirements.

How I Navigate Prospects towards Consultation on My Website

○ **A Needs Assessment Form:** This is the best first step. You are welcome to review mine: http://upscaleyourbusiness.com/needs-assessment-2/

○ **Calendar link to schedule consultation:** When a prospect clicks to submit their completed Needs Assessment Form, they are instantly redirected to my calendar link, TimeTrade (www.TimeTrade.com), to schedule their complimentary consultation, while simultaneously my email inbox shows me I have a prospect, and then an immediate follow-up email tells me the day and time of the scheduled consult—all in one fell swoop!

Section 2—Marketing and Promotion

"By publishing content that shows customers you understand their problems and can show them how to solve them, you build credibility."

~Ardath Albee, Author of Emarketing Strategies for the Complex Sale

Online Newsletter—Your Branded Platform

I am still a firm believer in the value of a company newsletter, even if these days fewer people read them, since so many items are being received in their inbox.

Provided your newsletter has great headlines and consistently appealing themes, your audience **will** read it**,** and as they become more familiar with you, they will actually look forward to receiving each new issue.

Initially, I emailed my newsletter every month, then every couple of months, and finally, when I had a steady flow of clients, I brought it down to four times a year, which I continue to do. Readers tell me it's a perfect frequency and a nice way to stay in touch.

Essential Newsletter Elements

What should be in your newsletter?

- **Obviously, your business name and company logo**.

- **Your company colors:** Your newsletter should match the overall look and feel of your brand, with the same colors as you have on your website. Using Colorcorp (http://colorcop.net/), a free download, you can get exact matches.

- **The date and the issue:** Print the month or season, "Autumn Edition," "Summer Edition," and always the year.

- **Articles:** I recommend you include at least two from this list of ideas:

  - **Your latest blog:** As your main article, you might use your latest blog post. Why reinvent the wheel? Why do two separate articles if you can get extra mileage out of one?

- Content from other writers: Share an article you found online or in a magazine and include some comments to highlight key points, or provide your personal insight, or highlight your expertise on the topic.

- Fillers: Education for your reader; slightly promotional too, but be mindful of striking the right balance. These could include client case studies (share how you've made an impact on their business), testimonials (this offers a way to let your clients share a personal experience of working with you). You can also share details about programs and packages you may be offering.

- **Links to relevant pages on your website and/or blog:** For example: "Click here for testimonials" or "Click here for my video interview."

- **Social media buttons:** Most newsletter services have made it very simple. All you have to do is type in your Twitter name or Facebook business page address and it will make the link for you.

- **Link to your email address:** Have it so that anyone who wants to contact you can click on that button and their email will open with your address populated right into the "To" field.

- **A special offer:** This can be particularly valuable when you're starting your business. An example would be one complimentary hour for every five hours purchased.

Finally, and very important, *test out* your newsletter by sending a draft to yourself, and click through the links to make sure they all work.

To learn more, visit www.UpscaleYourVirtualAssistantBusiness.com

Blogging

I've talked about networking in an earlier section, so now let's look at blogging and social media. These are not mutually exclusive strategies. They can work together beautifully to "marry" your marketing efforts and drive traffic to your website.

Why Blog?

- *O* **To show off your understanding of the needs of your audience:** Your blogging audience *always* includes potential clients, and there is no better way than "blogging" to have them see how *you can* relate to issues they have in their everyday business dealings. If you strike a chord with your blog, and have a link to your website, clients will come to you. If you do this on a regular basis, you rapidly increase your number of followers and potential for new business.

- *O* **To share new knowledge:** An example would be to talk about a product you have discovered that will help every small business.

- *O* **To share a personal experience:** This shows your human side and, mixed in with these other blogs, sheds a light on your personality, your humor, your sensitivity, etc. Your blog followers get a sense of who you are.

- *O* **To recycle interesting content:** For example, you can write an article for your newsletter, and then make it a blog post. From there you might develop five or six great tweets to link your readers back to your blog to read the full article. It's an enticing way to get people to follow your blog.

Pay attention to your writing skills, grammar, and punctuation. Your own well written blogs are a great way to show off your writing abilities, especially important if "writing" is a principal service you offer.

Finding Inspiration for your Newsletters and Blogs

Have a "topic" folder on your computer and add to it any time a newsletter or blog idea comes to mind or comes across your table.

If you are stuck for inspiration and don't have a great topic, gather ideas from other people's blogs/articles, maybe even from different industries. These are a few suggestions.

- **Rewrite:** Read a few articles on a similar topic and write about it in your own voice. Create a dynamic headline and put your own "spin" on it.

- **Interests of your target audience:** Get inspiration from magazines and other blog articles related to the interests of your target audience.

- **Personal experience:** Take something relevant that you're experiencing in your daily life, inject some humor, and address it in your blog post. It might even be something silly that happened with your child that you can then relate back to your business.

- **LinkedIn Group Discussions:** Join groups for your target market, and participate in discussions. This will always provide inspiration.

Social Media

Using social media to establish your credibility and highlight your expertise is an essential element in marketing your services. Since we are "virtual," its importance cannot be stressed enough.

Social media provides a supremely effective way to connect with people, develop relationships, and share information. You can grow your "following" of ideal clients using a variety of simple strategies: In my self-study program, described at the end of this book, there is a module devoted entirely to these strategies.

For example, by posting some of your original content and coupling this with sharing other people's relevant content, you can target your messages to your potential clients. Messages should educate, inform, provoke thought, or solve a problem. In essence you become a "filter" of overall business knowledge.

The best part is that once you know how to effectively use social media to grow your business, you can then offer it as a service to your clients, which will also enable you to charge higher rates.

Section 3—Open for Business

"We are what we repeatedly do. Excellence, therefore, is not an act but a habit."

~ Aristotle

Responding to Potential Clients

A potential client has been impressed enough by your marketing, social media, and/or website to make contact with you. To maintain their level of enthusiasm, it is just as important that you be equally impressive and dynamic at the next stages.

Your First Impression / Pre-Consultation

Set up expectations and intentions for the consultation in a manner that will keep the potential client engaged.

Unless you follow my earlier suggestion of a link on your website for clients to schedule their consultation, generally, the first contact with a new client will be via email. Have a template/standard script such as: "Thank you for contacting me and let's schedule a time to speak; here's a link to my calendar." If you don't have a calendar link such as TimeTrade, then offer a script such as: "Please propose some dates and times and I will confirm one that fits my schedule." You will eventually see a pattern of days/times that work best for you, at which point you can propose those. I personally find Tuesdays to Fridays, between 1:00 and 4:00 p.m. Eastern Standard Time the most convenient.

It shows efficiency to send a "Looking forward to our discussion" email. Confirm the date and time and who will be initiating the call. If you're calling, reiterate the phone number: "This is the number I will be calling to reach you." If they're calling, then remind them of your phone number.

To set up consultation expectations and to state the intentions of the conversation, in your email you would include wording along the lines: "During our discussion, I would like to understand what currently is not working for you in your business, what your priority projects are, and what expectations you have of a Virtual Assistant. I will address your specific support needs and be happy to discuss with you my rates and packages and how I work. We will then go over the next steps if you'd like to move forward."

Giving them this overview of what to expect sets the tone. I can share with you that as soon as I get on the phone with clients for the consultation, most dive into the discussion without any need for me to set it up, invariably expressing gratitude for the helpfulness of my prior communication.

I haven't inundated them with emails. I literally sent just one. But it's the professionalism in setting up the expectations that they're responding to. They knew what we would be discussing. They knew what to expect. They felt reassured about what was to come, and they hadn't even spoken with me yet.

They start thinking to themselves…if this is the way she operates **her** business, I certainly can rely on her to represent **my** business in a professional manner too. These first impressions—before you speak with a client—take on major significance. If, on the other hand, you handle this early interaction in a way that seems disorganized, it will reflect poorly as a first impression.

Consultation

You'll develop your own way to conduct the consultation…the following is what I do.

When I first get on the phone, I ask if this is still a convenient time. Although it most likely **is**, some people could be exceptionally busy. This courtesy is always appreciated and a great way to start a consultation.

I have tried a couple of different ways to proceed with the conversation. One early unsuccessful approach was along the lines: "I'm going to drive the discussion, and I'll tell you how I work and you can just respond to that." This approach was wrong because most potential clients want to go straight into their problems—to be *listened to*—and then to hear how they can be helped.

My best approach that has consistently worked is to begin with: "I'm going to let **you** drive the discussion, and I'll be taking notes; then I'll respond to your specific points with solid solutions."

Let's look at a client example: "I'm really struggling. I need to work on my newsletter. I also need some templates or scripts for dealing with my potential clients, and I'd like to have a system in place for follow-up with my prospects."

As they are speaking, I carefully note everything they're needing help with, and I respond: "I'm happy to address each of your points. I'm very experienced with newsletters, so I can either work *with you* on yours or can relieve you entirely of the burden and handle it *by myself*. Do you already have a service and a template set up?" Having produced many newsletters, I know I can proceed positively—even if I am unfamiliar with the service they use, as I can learn it—so my response will be: "Wonderful, I will be of great value to you with regard to your newsletter."

Now, I go to the next point: "As for your templates and scripts, both existing and future, a solution I offer is an Operations Manual, which I will create for you. Here we will keep all your templates and scripts in one place, along with every process, and then we will simply pick from them as needed. With this system too, your prospect follow-ups will be seamless, and clients will never be lost in the shuffle. This streamlining will help take your business to the next level."

A typical response is: "What a phenomenal idea! I love what you have to offer me—and you've addressed the specific areas where I need the most support."

At this point, I continue: "I'm now going to let you know about my pricing structure and billing arrangements, which I will confirm in an email along with my proposal outlining everything we've covered."

At the end, if I feel the client might be ready, I try to sign them up right away, and have been successful in doing so: "If you'd like to give me your credit card details, we could get started this week."

My main advice to VA's is to **listen intently** and take good notes, and always be ready to **impress the client early in the discussion** with smart ideas, such as the Operations Manual.

Handling Objections / Rejection

If your consultation had gone very well, but you were nevertheless rejected, a follow-up phone call might be worthwhile.

If the reason was that your rates were too high, you could ask, "What is your budget?" and then let them know what you can accomplish for them with that budget. "With your budget of X amount of dollars a month, I can provide you these services." Turn it around on them and you may find that you get their business.

Make the case too that you are the right person for them to hire, that you're not simply task-based, and you'll be proactive in helping them…not only to free up their time but also to **get more business**. That has worked for me. If you come across as a VA who's going to do not just what's being asked but will literally be hands on and presenting great ideas, and you can "sell" them on this, maybe even demonstrate it while on the phone, you have a good chance to win them over. Also, ask them to review your testimonials or contact your references.

Maintain your professionalism. If they decide not to work with you, don't take it personally and don't *show* that you are upset. You will find there are people who click with you and people who don't. And you can scratch your head and wonder why, but they have their own reasons. Just bless them and move on. "NEVER BURN A BRIDGE!" Sometimes they come back to you, as I have experienced more than once!

If you don't get to speak again after the consultation, prepare email responses for various scenarios. For example, if they say they have decided to hold off for the time-being, a standard template might be: "I appreciate you letting me know. Please contact me when you're ready." As you develop templates for each scenario, put them in your Operations Manual to copy and paste, and send as appropriate.

I believe in *always* acknowledging when someone writes to you, even if it's not good news. I've had people write, "I've decided to work with someone else." I simply write back, "I really appreciate the time you took in responding and I wish you the best of luck with your new Virtual Assistant. Please know that I'm here if I can support you at any time in the future."

That kind of a response and initiative can make all the difference. Quite possibly, you had a great consultation and they found you very professional, but they chose another VA simply based on price. As a result of your thoughtful response, they may even refer you to a colleague, and if their new VA doesn't work out, they may well come back to you. I have benefited in this way.

When I hire a VA for my team, I always notify the other applicants, and the ones who write, "I appreciate the time you took to speak with me, and I would be grateful if you will keep me in mind for any projects you may have in the future," have elevated their status in my book and, provided they were suitably qualified, are moved to the **very top of my list** of future hirees!

When It's a YES!

If you get a "YES" to your proposal and pricing, congratulations! Here is what I suggest you send to the client.

- *o* **"Getting Started with XYZ Virtual Assistant Company" email:** This covers the initial steps and information you require in order to begin working for the client. It should include their log-in information for their newsletter, social media accounts, and other platforms. I provide the client with an Excel spreadsheet to fill in, with rows for newsletter service, Facebook, Twitter, and LinkedIn, and columns for usernames, email addresses, passwords, etc.

- *o* **Agreement for Services:** Usually a standard document. Be sure to add in the client's name, any specific customization for the client, and terms of payment. You may also want to include a Payment Authorization form. (I strongly advise never to start client work before receiving some payment.)

- *o* **"Welcome" email:** This is a follow-up to acknowledge that you have received their signed agreement and thank them for their payment. Provide an outline of the projects that you discussed in your consultation. "Dazzle" them a little with: "Here's what we discussed, here are the projects, this is how I suggest we prioritize them, and I see the most important immediate task for me to work on as…."

- *O* **New Client Welcome Kit:** In today's world of the internet, mailing a welcome kit is a personal touch a client would never expect. Mine is an attractive package which includes hard copies of important documents previously emailed plus some free goodies with my business name. Clients love it and I get wonderful feedback.

Section 4—Keeping Your Clients

"Customer Service is awareness of needs, problems, fears and aspirations."

~ Elwin Hornedo

Characteristics and Traits You Need to Keep Your Clients

It is more difficult to fire an onsite employee than it is to fire a Virtual Assistant. It may be frivolous to say that "Virtual Assistants" are a dime a dozen, but there is *always* a choice—a new Virtual Assistant is easy to find. To keep your clients, you need to inspire loyalty and reasons for your clients to feel they can't do without you. You want to be their **hero**! Aside from your skills, expertise, and knowledge, what are the characteristics and traits you need to exhibit?

O **Integrity:** Be true to your word in everything that you do. If you say that you will have something to a client by Tuesday at 1 o'clock, make sure you do just that. Often, I remind clients—maybe two days before the due date—that I still plan to provide their project by the agreed date. If *for any reason* you can't have it completed on time, give the client as much notice as possible and let them know why, and provide an alternative solution if you can. Also, never mislead a client. If you lose integrity, you lose your client.

O **Reliability:** Several of my clients worked previously with other qualified Virtual Assistants, but things were falling through the cracks…clients found themselves having to "keep tabs" on their VA or hold their hand. This is the last thing clients want to be doing. Never lose sight of the fact that they are paying for your service so they can **move on** to other things; they **do not** want to be checking on you—they want to **rely** on you, and if they can, you will likely be *indispensable*.

O **Accuracy:** You have to be conscious of accuracy *in every task that you perform*. Mistakes and typos are unacceptable. Once your clients see that they don't have to check your work, you save them *precious* time, and this they value highly.

O **Upbeat Personality:** Be cheerful, be positive, be enthusiastic, be willing, be uplifting, be reassuring, show confidence, and create a rapport with your client and with their clients if your responsibilities include such contact. You are a support for your client, and *your disposition* plays a major role in their view of you.

O **Resourcefulness:** If your client doesn't know how to do something or where to obtain information, be their "go-to resource." If they ask for your help, make sure you get them their answer, whatever it takes. And if a client mentions something simply in passing, like, for example: "I probably would benefit from a business magazine," give them some magazine names you know, and if there's more you can research for them or you come across an article, think: "Let me send this over to Carol, because we talked about that the other day." Just be that person who thinks about your clients even when you're not in their presence or when you're not speaking with them. If anything useful pops up that was talked about in the past, bring the subject up again: "Remember our discussion about *such and such* topic? I found a great resource for you…." This way, you are creating a mindset that impresses clients.

O **Follow-Through and Follow-Up:** Stay on top of, and see through to the end, *everything* you are expected to accomplish.

An example of a basic follow-up might be "circling back" with a client if you've sent something and not received their required feedback. Even if they were satisfied with the work you did, it shows your level of commitment in not allowing any project to fall off the radar. Being a minor "pest" in such cases wins praise—every time.

Another example, if you've not spoken with your client in a while and have been left to your own devices, would be to send an email with an update and overview of their projects and tasks you've been working on. This kind of unasked initiative means so much to a client and creates loyalty.

o **Work well under pressure:** Never tell your clients about your workload with other clients or in any way imply that you're overwhelmed. Ideally each client should *feel like* they're your *only* client...*even though* they know in reality that not to be the case. I advise against taking on more work than you can handle, unless you have other VA's you can trust, who will work with you. If pressure overcomes you, take a break and meditate or go for a short walk. VA's who find or learn ways to handle stress get more work done and inspire confidence, and this is noticed by clients, whereas an obviously stressed VA will be of concern to clients. There are many good books on managing stress.

o **Ability to multi-task:** Super important! You have to be able to take on three, four, or five different projects for a client or for **several** clients, and maintain **all** of them. It's not easy, but it can be achieved if you have efficient systems and an organized mind.

o **Willingness to learn:** Don't tell a client you don't know how to do something if it is something you can learn. A client requested, "I would like you to take my spreadsheet data and turn it into a graph." I had no idea **how** to do this. However, I responded, "No problem." Why did I say that without hesitation? Because I knew I would find the answer with the help of my trusted friend, Google. I simply typed into the

Google search bar, "How do I turn spreadsheet data into a graph?" The process was really simple, I retained the client and learned something new that I have used many times since, both for myself and for other clients.

Always be secure in turning to Google. It's a free and very valuable resource; you will be amazed at how much knowledge you will find there. Also YouTube—not just for watching silly cats and babies—offers a wealth of videos that answer all kinds of business-related questions.

○ **Willing to teach:** If you've learned something that will help clients in their business, tell them about it; offer to give them detailed instructions. There are tools to record videos on your screen—where you can explain and demonstrate new processes—which you will then send your clients. You can also share your computer screen with them in real time, and they can watch your steps while you perform them. Clients love to learn anything new of value to their business and especially appreciate a VA willing to be open to teaching them. When you show yourself to be someone who is a resource for just about everything that they know nothing about, you are treasure!

○ **An "ideas" person:** Be proactive and offer suggestions where you see the opportunity to make improvements in any area of a client's business. It may be something little or major, but you must be confident it is practical, financially feasible, and that the client will be receptive to the idea coming from you. When clients see there is more to you than a VA who simply carries out assignments, you become more *valuable*.

○ **Help to grow the client's business:** If you consistently prove effective in taking over tasks that free up your clients'

To learn more, visit www.UpscaleYourVirtualAssistantBusiness.com

time, so they can focus more on activities that increase their income, **you are gold!** If you are able yourself to *create extra income for them,* **you are priceless!**

Closing Comments

Congratulations! You've made it this far and you've learned about:

- Getting started, including set-up costs and required equipment and skills;

- Strategies for Branding your business and where and how to network and share about your VA services;

- Marketing and Promotion, including website elements, newsletter essentials, and blogging;

- "Open for Business" strategies, including how to respond to potential clients, set up of your pre-consultation, conduct the consultation, and steps to take in getting your prospect on the path toward working with you.

- Keeping your clients, the characteristics you need beyond the skills.

With this foundation, you will be able to have your ideal clients recognize you as an expert in your field: by winning them over in the pre-sales phase via your website, social media, and marketing; by demonstrating consistency in follow-up and follow-through; and by informing them of specific ways you will be able to help them streamline their processes, increase their business, and reduce their stress. You will have clients who will feel "lucky" to get to work with you and who likely will provide referral business.

If you have passion for administrative work and you're organized and resourceful, this is a great business to be in. It is a fast-growing and competitive industry, so it's really about how successful you can be *in setting yourself apart.*

The times when I had trouble making ends meet or getting new clients or keeping the clients I had—*as I look back*—were actually a blessing: I was forced into being more creative and innovative. By *experimenting* with many different strategies and processes, and attending numerous seminars, I ultimately came up with the right formulas to market a VA business successfully, run it optimally, meet and exceed client expectations…and make an excellent living at it.

What I have learned and I share in this book, I cover in greater detail and with more topics in my **"Upscale Your Virtual Assistant Business VIP Platinum Self-Study Program"** (see page 54). Together with this book, the Self-Study program will save new and struggling Virtual Assistants countless hours and considerable heartache.

Those of you only needing help with **specifically targeted** aspects of the business are invited to schedule a complimentary consultation to discuss private mentoring via this link: http://bit.ly/VAMentorConsult

I appreciate your taking the time to read my book…whether you are considering a career as a Virtual Assistant, just starting out in the industry, or have been a VA for a while, and have found yourself struggling to get and keep clients, I hope you have found it helpful.

If you have any questions, don't hesitate to reach out. You can connect with me via the following:

- Email Jaimie@UpscaleYourBusiness.com

- Facebook: www.Facebook.com/UpscaleYourBusiness

- Twitter: www.Twitter.com/UpscaleYourBiz

- LinkedIn: https://www.linkedin.com/in/JaimieSkultety

- Google+: https://plus.google.com/+JaimieSkultetyUYB/posts

- Pinterest: http://www.pinterest.com/UpscaleYourBiz/

- Ph/Fax: 877-798-7701 | Skype: JMG52869

I look forward to furthering our connection. In the meantime, I wish you all the best and ongoing success,

VALUABLE BONUS *you weren't expecting...surprise your clients too!*

I wrote *"99 Ways to Outsource Your Way to Success"* as a valuable giveaway on my website. Click here and it's yours: http://bit.ly/99WaysToOutsourceYourWayToSuccess. You can customize it with your own branding and logo. Offer it on social media and/or your website. *"99 ideas"* of what to outsource could be the "spark" that gets prospects to **outsource** to you, *becoming new clients* **and** *a source of funds to purchase my Self-Study program!* As email addresses have to be supplied to receive *"99 ways,"* you will have the benefit too of being able to build up an email list to use for all your future marketing.

Upscale Your Virtual Assistant Business VIP Platinum Self-Study Program

If you're interested in learning more about being a VA, marketing your services, and managing your pipeline of prospects…I invite you to review my VIP Platinum Self-Study Program, specifically for VA's who want to optimize their business. Here is just a very small sample of what is included:

- ❖ How to use Social Media to promote your services;

- ❖ Effective follow-up strategies after you send your proposal if you do not hear back;

- ❖ What to include in your Welcome Kit;

- ❖ How to set up clients in your "system" and how to "ramp up" with them;

- ❖ How to manage communication with your clients;

- ❖ How to use Outlook to stay on top of your tasks;

- ❖ And so much more!

The program consists of 6 video modules, transcripts, workbooks, and templates, 2 (60-minute) 1:1 private coaching calls with me, and comes with 11 bonuses, which include checklists as well as step-by-step and done-for-you items that enable you to get your business structure and systems into place quickly. It also offers "recommended" assignments to help advance your progress, plus access to my Private Facebook Online Forum, where you will find ongoing support, recommendations, and resources.

For the complete overview, and to register for the program, please visit: www.UpscaleYourVirtualAssistantBusiness.com.

• • •

One-on-One Coaching: If you are a new or struggling VA, and are trying to figure out why you are not achieving the success you strive for, or are uncertain how to take your business to the next level, or you simply desire to add to your VA skills…as an alternative to the self-study program, I will diagnose which areas of your VA business we need to focus on and address these specifically in one-on-one coaching. Use this link to schedule a complimentary consultation: http://bit.ly/VAMentorConsult

About The Author

Jaimie Skultety is owner of Upscale Your Business, a company providing Virtual Assistant and Social Media Marketing Services to Solo Entrepreneurs, Professional Coaches, and Consultants. She has been featured on Forbes.com, South Florida Business Spotlight, Savvy Biz Woman Magazine, Professional Association of Résumé Writers and Career Coaches Spotlight, Paycheck to Passion Podcast, and Gables Home Page.

With over 25 years administrative, management, and marketing experience, Jaimie stays current on the latest in social media trends and business technology. This wide-ranging experience, coupled with her innate organizational talents, has allowed her to implement and manage systems, structures, and procedures which maximize the efficiency of her clients' businesses **and** helps them increase their bottom line. Jaimie has also written several articles relating to business administration and social media.

Jaimie offers her VIP Platinum Self-Study Program "Upscale Your Virtual Assistant Business" for other Virtual Professionals who want to optimize their business.

She will soon launch her newest product: "Social Media Acceleration Suite—A Complete Roadmap to Have Your Ideal Clients Chasing You."

Jaimie resides in Boynton Beach, Florida, is married to Steve, an Industrial Designer (http://www.I-DrawDesign.com). They have a son, Spencer. Aside from work, Jaimie enjoys participating in Scout activities, spending time with family, cooking, Scrabble, and Words with Friends.

Websites Owned and Operated by Jaimie Skultety:

http://www.UpscaleYourBusiness.com

http://www.EndtheFeastorFamineCycle.com

http://www.UpscaleYourVirtualAssistantBusiness.com

www.ingramcontent.com/pod-product-compliance
Lightning Source LLC
Chambersburg PA
CBHW051224170526
45166CB00005B/2028